Mississippi Sounds

Mississippi Sounds

The 1949-1963 story of a family of six that
moved from city to small town–
New Orleans to Pascagoula, Mississippi–
and the amazing events as
family grew to eight

IRA HARKEY

To order additional copies of this book, contact:

Xlibris Corporation
1-888-795-4274
www.Xlibris.com
Orders@Xlibris.com

22986

Contents

This writing is for Bobi, Meg,

Erik, Maybin, Amelie, Dale and

the memory of their mother

Marie Ella Levert Gore Harkey

The 1949-1963 story of a family of six that moved from city to small town – New Orleans to Pascagoula, Mississippi – and the amazing events as family grew to eight

PROLOGUE

It was August in 1949. So densely packed was the crowd in the auto that it resembled photos of Oakies fleeing the dust bowl in the 1930s American West. Main difference was that this car didn't have a mattress and a chair tied onto its top.

Trekking east were Mama and Papa and their four children, two dogs and one cat. These latter three were chosen unwisely as fellow travelers. Their barking, hissing, snarling, howling and dashing back and forth frantically from window to window entertained the children. For grownups it intensified the vision of hell they were glimpsing.

Also jammed into the station wagon were suitcases, carry bags, clothes hangers, laundry bags, cardboard and plywood boxes, paper bags, every conceivable thing with an opening that could be stretched to take more stuff.

Driving was Ira Harkey, 31, newspaperman, veteran of Navy service in World War II, who six months before had realized the dream of every city reporter one day to run a small town paper. He had left the employ of the New Orleans Times-Picayune to take over the weekly Chronicle-Star of Pascagoula Mississippi.

Beside him was his wife Marie Ella Gore, unhappy at being taken from the social whirl of her city to the unknown of a "two bit town" on the Mississippi Sound. She had extracted a promise from her husband that if she were unhappy after three years in the "sticks," they would move back to New Orleans. To be truthful, Ira would have promised anything and trusted providence to cover for him.

Competing with the animal noise was pandemonium created by the three young children in the back of the station wagon. Erik, seven, fair skinned and blue eyed, curly golden hair was constantly teasing, ordering and tormenting three-year-old Maybin, already the headstrong imaginative little devil he would become, husky, straight brown hair, olive skin.

The third back seater, Meg, ten, contributed to the turbulence in the rear by continuously ordering Erik and Maybin to stop it right now, orders they didn't even hear it seemed. Ordinarily ladylike, the blonde, pretty Meg was the younger children's frustrated good-manners teacher.

Fourth offspring in the rear was Ira III, a big boy of twelve, who resembled Maybin more than the others, in looks, not behavior. He sat quietly watching the flat landscape slide by. Once or twice he joined the others in asking the prevailing question, "Are we there yet, Daddy?" and, "When will we get there, Daddy?"

Papa pulled over to the side of the road, turned around facing the back and announced, "The next time any one of you asks any question about getting there, I'm going to stop and paddle all of you." They must have believed him – a little – because the infuriating questions slacked off to only two more. (No paddling)

The moving ordeal did not stop with arrival of the mob at the rented summer house on the Pascagoula beach. Whining from the uncomfortable trip, the youngsters had to be pushed to help unload. There was material to set up for sleeping. Other furnishings would arrive by van later.

The house, a comfortable looking cottage, sat about 100 feet from the beach boulevard. The one story had a porch along its front, half of it screened. A wide central hallway ran down the middle, broadening toward the end into a large crossway dining hall. Four bedrooms, one at each corner of the dining space, with a kitchen protruding from one side, were ample for the six new residents. Across the rear was another screened porch.

A hundred feet behind the house was a two-story structure – two car garage with two-room living quarters above.

The land was four or five feet above the average level of the Gulf in the front, fairly good protection from surging hurricane-driven waters. The property ran from Beach Boulevard 600 feet inland to Washington Avenue. It was dotted with more than thirty producing pecan trees.

The owner was a member of an old local family, then living in Mobile. He would not even listen to an offer to buy.

Amelie, nine; Meg, 17

HEREWITH AMELIE'S TALE

"Hurry up, Daddy." Amelie said to me, "we have to go call on the Blessed Virgin."

It was the day before Easter in April 1960 at our hotel in Hendersonville, North Carolina. Amelie, eight years old, was anxious to go to visit the director of her sister Meg's school. She had forgot the title "reverend mother," but she knew that it was something impressive, so she chose the most impressive of all.

Amelie, an energetic, bright, yellow haired little beauty, was wise beyond her years. Number 5 in our string of children, Amelie was the first of the siblings to be born in Mississippi.

Lee (her nickname) and her father (me) had flown up to St. Genevieve of the Pines school in Hendersonville. The flights were Lee's first airplane rides and she was impressed with the big Constellation that we rode from Mobile to Atlanta, unhappy with the bouncing DC-3 we rode to Asheville, and outraged to find that on her ticket she was listed as "Master Lee Harkey."

"I hate boys," she told a stewardess.

At Genevieve we found Meg to be a woman of 17 now, poised and confident but a bit sad at nearing the end of the days at the school. She had done well in her studies, made several firm friends and grown close to some of the nuns. Mother Potts, school director and erstwhile "blessed virgin," was a favorite. Accompanied by Meg, she took Lee and me on a walking tour of the school and its lovely rolling tree-covered grounds.

The mountains of western North Carolina were spectacular. After enduring the harshest winter in history, they were spending extra effort to make this spring their loveliest.

Cherry trees were solid with blossoms, blankets of wild flowers sunned themselves on the hillsides, tulips and pansies bloomed and everywhere the forsythia showed its glorious yellow. Lee chattered her pleasure at the beauty of it all, new to her.

On Saturday in a rented car we drove some exciting miles along the Blue Ridge Parkway. We stopped by a summer camp I attended 30 years before. "Lee," Meg said, "Daddy spent the summer here when he was a little boy."

"And it's still standing," Lee exclaimed. "Gee!"

We drove through the Pisgah National Forest, surely one of the country's most beautiful, and back on the Parkway's unfinished stretches. More than once Lee buried her face in Meg's lap as we edged around 290-degree curves with nothing to our right but thin air.

Alas, even here we encountered that detestable nuisance, the motorized teenaged jerk. A specimen roared up behind us in a clanking junk heap. He was our annoying company for miles, as here there was no room to pull over and let him clank off to spoil some other innocent pleasure seekers' drive.

Meg stayed two nights with us in the hotel. Once as I told them goodnight and closed their door I heard Lee whisper, "Daddy's nice, isn't he, Meg?"

Wages a king might grovel for.

Amelie came off the press on 25 May 1951. A nurse exited the delivery room and said, "Twin boys for the Harkeys!" You could have knocked me over with a diaper. When she saw the shock she'd caused she hurriedly said, "No. It's a wee girl." Members of the family uncrossed their fingers. They wanted a girl and there she was. The menage now included three boys and two girls, a full house. Reaction was varied among the siblings, out on the hospital lawn at feeding time to catch a glimpse of their small new relative. A nurse held her up at the window.

> Maybin: Daddy, is it a real one?
> Erik: That little thing!
> Meg: She's real cute. She looks
>   like me.

Bobi: She doesn't have any hair.
          I want a boy.

I loved her instantly. She looked exactly like me.

Lee was less than four when it became apparent she was a take-over character. She kept her playthings separate from those of the others. She insisted on doing what she wanted and when she wanted to, benign and harmless activities.

Little brother Dale was born sixteen months after she was, and it was not long before it was clear that she would be his mentor. She was always by his side, protecting him, directing him. They were a pair.

At that age Amelie talked incessantly, about what, no one could tell.

To our surprise Amelie proved to be a daredevil equal to her older brother Maybin. At only four we once found her 20 feet off the ground on the flat roof of the house we built in 1955. We learned later of the ingenious way that she climbed to the roof, a difficult job for anyone without a long ladder.

With Maybin's help, she placed an empty milk bottle upside down at the back entrance to the house. She stepped on the bottle end, from there to a rail of the entrance structure. The door was then held open by brother Maybin for Lee to step on the doorknob, then the knocker. From there she stepped to the top of the door and used a niche in the wall to gain the roof.

When I found her atop the house, I was almost too choked with fear to try to coax her back down. No need to, Dad. When I called to her she came to the edge of the roof and whisked to the ground as agile as a monkey. If Maybin had let the door slip, or even moved it a fraction, Lee could have pitched to the ground. She said the perilous assent was Maybin's idea. "Who, me?" he asked.

One day baby Lee told me she had "toop" for lunch.

"Was it good, your toop?"

"Toop, Daddy, toop."

"Oh, toop."

"No, Daddy. Toop!"

"That's what I said. Toop!"

"Tooo-ooo-ooo-p," Amelie shrieked.

Now my teasing was verging on cruel. I said, "All right, baby, you had soup, eh?"

"Yes. Toop." She turned and toddled away, turned back to look at me. "Toop, Daddy."

I learned something by this session. Lee says toop for soup, hearing soup. But to her ears toop said by others is not soup. Older persons must say soup to mean toop. Enough.

At two, Amelie brought home a cat, a woebegone tortoise-shell type. It occupied its time fending off Amelie's expressions of affection. It laced a new red streak on her face whenever it could get in a lick.

This next Lee – ism I've gone through with other children, but it still challenges my gag reflex. I walked into the kitchen and found two-year-old Lee lying on the floor eating dinner with our dog Susy at the dog's bowl.

Amelie came to spend the night with me in the motel to which I had moved when she was seven. She performed for me her school cheerleaders' routine, every word, every move. "I watch the cheerleaders," she told me, "instead of the players." She brought with her a tooth that she had just lost. She let me know that a friend of hers had received a dollar from the tooth fairy instead of the prevailing dime. I told her that was too much to expect of a fairy. Anyway, she found a dollar under her pillow on waking. Thus do fairies spoil little girls.

When she was nine she remonstrated, "Daddy, I'm always writing you love letters but you never write any to me." I said that if she would consult old Chronicles she would find that in my column I wrote love letters to her for nine years, since the May day she came off the presses in 1951.

Lee was precocious mentally as well as physically. At nine months she had eight teeth which Mama bragged about one evening. Maybin asked, "Does she bite?" She was such a spirited dear from age three to ten that her antics if lined up without comment would reach from here to there.

She got so enthusiastic while writing her letter to Santa Claus when she was five that Daddy had to suggest a halt. "All right, Daddy," she agreed. But she figured a continuation a few minutes later, came back and said, "Daddy, I'm ready now to write the bunny rabbit."

When she was five she inherited two very small puppies from a friend. She cuddled them every moment when she was home. One night she could not be found to be put to bed. She was not missing any sleep, however. We found her in the yard curled up with the puppies sound asleep.

I asked her when she was six, "Lee, why did you paint nail polish all over Meg's jewelry box?"

"I DID NOT DO IT."

"Come now, Lee. If you didn't do it, who did?"

"I DID NOT DO IT, DADDY. If you don't believe me, you can ask God." Not having any kind of communication in that direction, I had to drop the inquisition.

Amelie's daring made me depart the club swimming pool when she showed up with her mother. Lee was allowed to climb up to the high diving board from which the two-foot-tall doll would jump time after time scaring old rough-tough father. It was all right that she loved also to stand on my shoulders as I walked around a room with her unsupported except by her own balance. Meg had done this years before when she was a toddler.

At the table Lee said one dinner time, "Daddy, do you know Dale holds his nose when he eats the squash, so he won't taste it?"

"I don't have to hold my nose, cause I have a cold."

Amelie's quick intelligence, her original creativity, the fun of just being with her, would make a simple listing of her events delightfully amusing.

One day after I had moved into a motel, Lee came to lunch with me. She told me that after lunch I was to take her to Mrs. Possom's house to play with Laura. Lee gave me directions as we drove and once there I recognized it as the Parson's home. Parson's, Possum's, fun all the same.

One afternoon when she was five I saw her on the telephone, glued to it. An irritated Maybin, standing by, said she's been on the phone for an hour and would not give it up. He finally grabbed the phone and after a short battle held it triumphantly over Lee's head. "Lee, you know we share everything here. All of us, even the phone. You know that Lee."

"I DO NOT!" she shrilled sternly, leaping to try to catch the phone in Maybin's grasp.

A few days later I had a second telephone installed in the house for the exclusive use of the children. This was not a show-off move, as claimed by some unfriendly people. It was a peace keeper and a move to allow the grownups in and out phone access.

Amelie was married in 1968 at 17, just after graduating from high school. The groom, Rex Foster, lived in Gautier, a tiny settlement across the west mouth of the Pascagoula River. Rex was 18. I wondered how long such a marriage could last. Answer: in 2004, after 37 years, it was lasting well.

Rex graduated from college in only three years. When he enrolled I worried that maybe he'd take it easy and need five years. He's not that kind of man. He is an agent for State Farm Insurance and has shown his prowess at selling life policies by winning many trips abroad for Amelie and himself.

The Fosters have two daughters, a son, three grandchildren and live at Gautier. At 52 Lee is a five-foot doll, her beauty so well preserved that no one could correctly guess her age.

Bobi at 12

HEREWITH BOBI'S TALE

His mother tried to teach Bobi to say "Ira B," which was part of his name. He was christened Ira B. Harkey III. The best the boy could say was something like Bob-ee. She wrote it Bobi, which looked like a proper Cajun nickname.

Born in New Orleans' Baptist Hospital on 15 November 1939, Bobi was alive during all of the US' part in World War II. The nearest he got to the war was a year spent at a Navy air station in Kansas to which his father was assigned.

Bobi was a sturdy, serious boy. From the beginning he grew so fast that he was put on a slimming diet before he could walk. Padding was removed from his playpen where he spent most of his time. The pediatrician said that lying on the wood would "harden up" his cushiony body.

Two years later the pediatrician spoke of a far more serious condition as weeping parents and grandparents heard him describe rheumatic fever which he said Bobi suffered from. A strep infection that could dangerously affect the heart in later life, it was difficult to treat before penicillin was in wide use. We were told that Bobi must be kept immobile for a year. He didn't tell how to keep a three-year-old boy immobile for even one day. Bobi's mother did a marvelous job in achieving near immobility.

Bobi and the family were fortunate. Many rheumatic fever victims suffer heart ills through life. Bobi did not. He played team football from pee-wees through junior high and high school to his annual college freshman-sophomore game.

When Bobi was eight, he and his father began playing catch with a baseball and kicking and passing with a football on weekends in Audubon Park. Passers-by would stop to watch a little kid kicking 30 and 35 yards. Later as a 192 pound high school fullback he averaged 42 yards his last two years. In one amazing show, beating unbeaten Biloxi 9-0, Bobi averaged an unbelievable 52 yards on nine punts.

His powerful punting raised interest in him by Alabama, Mississippi State, Stanford and Notre Dame. The Notre Dame scout told me that it was too bad that Bobi didn't have the intense interest to play that college football factories wanted. Good, I thought, not "too bad."

As a boy, he loved the life at summer camps. At his first one he wrote home that "I'm having a grand time, we had a swimming test yesterday and I past it. I know about ten boys, the ones in my cabin are Robert Soniat, Kenneth Kolb, Joe Goldstein and one dumb-bell who said America was discovered in 1948 and said Truman's name was Eisenhower. Love, Bobi."

When he came home from camp in 1952 he noticed a familiar protuberance at his mother's stomach. "Mama," he said, "if you have another baby I'm leaving home."

"So am I, my boy," she answered. She stayed and in September the family was graced with the arrival of William Millsaps Trousdale.

Bobi suffered through a crisis during his 10th year. "Daddy," he said one day, "I don't want to grow up to be a man."

All Papa could think to answer that was a joking, "What do you want to grow up to be, a woman?"

"No. I just don't want to be a man and not be able to play with my friends and have fun."

"Your friends are going to grow up, Bobi, and if you stay a boy you won't be able to play with them."

Papa gave him a full blast philosophical lecture about life's inevitable changes and how, as he grows older other things come along that are "fun." It didn't take. Bobi remained disconsolate for a while.

Bobi began piano lessons when he was 10 and by 13 showed an extraordinary talent with a "big touch" almost as powerful as a man's. The family excitement over him died sadly when Bobi reached 14 and his fellow athletes heaped scorn on his "sissy" activity. I told Bobi that almost all famous pianists were men, bought him albums, articles and books about them, all to nothing. He gave in to the taunting and shelved his talent.

The young family – parents, Bobi and younger sister – spent a short time together during the war while papa, an ensign, taught ground school at Olathe Naval Air Station in Kansas. It was a primary base where cadets were first taught to fly in the famous (or infamous) Yellow Peril biplanes that flew all day. At lunchtime one day Bobi and father were outside when a swarm of planes flew overhead. An excited Bobi called, "Look Daddy, planes come home for lunch!"

Well after the war in 1952, Bobi and I reached notable milestones. My first born reached the teens at 13. It was a signal event for the old man who had not felt old since he returned to college in 1939 three years older than his classmates.

I took Bobi and stood with him before a mirror and accused him of tiptoeing. He wasn't. He was standing flat footed on size 11-D feet, reaching an altitude only an inch below me. Those feet and the rest of him were testimonials to cod liver oil, vitamins, this and that and the wonders of the pediatric art. Heredity could not have done this because his forebearers on all sides were the briefest of men.

There was a time it seemed only weeks ago when this strapping boy was a spheroid infant gurgling in his playpen. Now he stood beside me almost a man – his face lean and shining, two budding pimples on his nose and a chin dress of fine light hairs glistening in the shine of the overhead light. He looked just like me.

Bobi finished at Pascagoula High School and entered Tulane in 1958. Not brilliant, he was a plugger who always "got it." He was the only freshman pledge to Delta Kappa Epsilon who earned good enough grades to be initiated that first year.

Bobi was graduated in 1962, served two years in the Navy and attended the University of Missouri's vaunted school of journalism. There he won a European trip to study the Common Market and NATO, placing his reports in various US and European newspapers.

A typical old-time traveling newspaperman, he worked in Florida, Iowa, Indiana, Missouri and at the New Orleans Times-Picayune and the States-Item. He then joined the public relations department of Ingalls Shipbuilding in Pascagoula, the largest industrial establishment in Mississippi.

He and his second wife, Lil Carter, and two beautiful and talented daughters have lived in Ocean Springs, Mississippi since 1978. He retired in 2002 and is working on a book about his great-grandfather Jean Baptiste Levert, affluent sugar plantation owner and leading New Orleans businessman.

Bobi and his wife Lil know how to manage money, a rarity in anyone under 80 nowadays. He and the family have traveled widely in the US and Canada, and have made several tours in Europe. Bobi is a practicing Catholic and chairman of his daughters' school board.

Known as a "solid citizen," he has earned wide respect for his exemplary life.

FATHER at 5

HEREWITH
FATHER'S TELL-TALE

Being an integral part of this account, the old man now drops his habitual modesty, steps from the shadows into the light and comments on this and that as his children grew from infancy to boyhood or girlhood. Organization of material is not chronological but is dictated by whimsy.

After several years of bravely withstanding my children's pleas, yells, tears, rages and mute, cold glares, I had a television receiver installed. That was in 1955.

The staunch holdout was because I believed teevee would consume too much of their time, that there would be too bitter a struggle to drag them away for meals and studying.

We must report that the children are being pretty sensible about the thing, but the old man is the butt of the current prevailing joke in the domicile.

As each child walks in, the greeting is something like this: "Humph! I thought you didn't like television, Daddy."

I'm sitting there before that insidious machine, program after program, hour after hour, my eyeball is hanging out on the end of my nose, a maniac grin on my face, sitting, sitting, sitting like a boneless idiot.

* * * *

To the tumult and shouting at our house in the early 1950s were added the wail of an anguished clarinet and the growl of an abused cornet. Meg, twelve, and Erik, nine, had received the tools for the band at school. For five days we endured the unholy noise of unmelodic squawks. We consulted band director Pat Rooney about at least giving them a tune to work on. Maybe we could stand that better than the disconnected instrument sounds ruining our days and nights. Even better, Pat coaxed them away from the machines. Meg and Rik saved their breath and we saved our sanity.

* * * *

We had fifty plus pecan trees in our deep yard. Enough volunteer nuts were produced that when gathered and sold would pay property taxes. My children saw me wielding a pick-up stick and insisted on joining me in the fun. The sticks have at their ends a round spiral of light metal. When the spiral is pressed against a grounded pecan, the wires spread to surround the nut. Raise the stick, the wires close and the pecan is captured. It so happened that I had four more sticks. Whee, what fun it was, what camaraderie, a new sport!

After that first year of fun, I couldn't cajole, threaten or frighten Meg, Erik and Maybin into helping me.

A year later a local business man came with a helper to harvest the nuts on the empty lot next door to ours. Watching were my former pecan pickers-up. Incredibly, to me that is, they grabbed sticks and began poking away when the businessman said he would let them join him. Fun to help him, drudgery to help me.

* * * *

Snoops were real bothers during the building of the new house. One cost us money, others brought us amusement. Flooring workers finished the exacting job of fitting slate floors one Friday. Over the weekend an unknown visitor walked over the floors, destroying the tediously paced patterns. It all had to be done over. At almost the very second we moved in a passerby came up to a family group inside and asked, "What's going on here?"

About the same time a snooper who evidently had stopped before, saw a group inside, came in and wandered about, and went upstairs. He reached the master bedroom. "What are you all doing up here," he asked the startled occupants. They were in bed.

* * * *

I'm not griping, understand, but the father of six sometimes feels life is like a Laocoon wrestling match not against two but a school of snakes. There is no escaping the demands to do this, that or the other when he'd rather do otherwise.

In my case I had PTAs, piano recitals, glee club recitals, pee-wee football, junior high football, B-team football, varsity football games, games, games, meetings, meetings, meetings. In 1955 there was one night on which I was expected to attend five important functions. I made two.

* * * *

In the 1950s I had for twenty years been under the impression that I was quite a performer on the diving board. The impression stems from my winning a medal in a YMCA diving match for 55-inch boys in the 30s.

That qualified me as an expert. The satisfied feeling of knowing all about diving remained with me over the decades, despite the fact that, although I frequently ran across diving boards here and there, I never again put foot on one.

One night at a Pascagoula pool, succumbing to a small-boy spirit of bravado, I assayed a jack-knife. The jack-knife was fine as far as it went, which was entirely too far. I sprang upward from the high board, reached a good height, and snapped into the jack-knife.

Thereafter, I set a new record, not for the beauty of the dive but for its duration. I maintained the folded position up, down, under and right to the bottom of the pool. It wasn't the best jack-knife ever done at that pool, but there is no doubt that was the longest.

As I disappeared in the locked position under the surface, so also disappeared my fond belief of diving prowess. It's a shame for a man to lose such a comforting illusion at my time of life. Besides, I haven't been able to turn my head or bend at the waist since.

Meg

HEREWITH
MEG'S TALE

The letters M E G are the initials of her three names, Marie Ella Gore. She was named for her mother after arriving at Baptist Hospital in New Orleans on 15 December 1941.

Old timers and history readers will recognize that date as eight days after the Japanese attacked Pearl Harbor and we entered World War II. The birth was welcomed with joy. The baby looked like all babies and she grew into a beautiful curly haired, sprightly, intelligent girl who was kind and fun to be with. In a conversation with a friend when she was ten, she said,

Meg: My Daddy doesn't come home for lunch on Thursday.
Friend: Why?

Meg.	We have liver then. He's allergic to liver.
Friend:	What's allergic?
Meg:	That means he doesn't like it.

Meg was the first of my two fearless females. As a tiny child she liked to stand on my shoulders without holding while I walked about. And she applauded the old man's humor, laughing appreciatively at such as, "Daddy, why don't you go swimming with us?"

"Because the water gets between my toes. I don't like that."

Meg seemed to grow up in a way different from the others. As the first girl, the oldest except Bobi, she assumed a role of authority that the younger ones accepted more or less. More or less means just that – her leadership was acknowledged sometimes, sometimes not. She was quiet. She grew tall, tall that is for a Southern girl, five feet seven inches, willowy and handsome. She distinguished herself within the family as a letter writer, expressing herself with the pen more often than not. She looked just like me.

At nine, her take charge attitude led her to reporting to her parents regularly the ebb and flow of events and of her efforts to keep order while they were absent. Her room was next to Maybin's in the new home into which we moved in 1955, six years after we came to Pascagoula. One night, returning from a party, we found one of Meg's frequent notes on the night table and herself asleep in our bed.

"I'm going to sleep in your bed because Maybin is coughing and I can't sleep. I gave him some water and tried to give him some stugh, red stugh. Love, Meg." The "stugh" mentioned, "red stugh" was Benadryl.

Returning home at night we looked forward to reading Meg's report on the state of the domicile. One was:

> We have been very good. Dillie (sitter) will tell you that We have been good. Dillie says you should give me a fine birthday present. [self plug]
>
> We played football. Dillie told us some stories. Bobi and Erik are in bed. Sammy [large black male dog] is sitting by the fire.

Susy [small brown female dog] is
on my bed.

Don't you just love that cozy animal picture with Susy on the bed, Sammy by the fire?

At age twelve our junior miss turned into perpetual motion. She flew off in all directions, arriving at no original destination because she kept changing it. She was studying tap dancing, piano, ballroom dancing, playing softball, active in the Girl Scouts and reading magazines she subscribed to. We usually saw her only as a breathless participant rushing in to change clothes for yet another performance.

Meg began piano lessons with Bobi and like him became a family virtuoso. She progressed rapidly and was accepted as a piano pedagogy student when later she entered Loyola university in New Orleans. Early marriage, moving about the country, children, all combined to reduce piano time to nothing and the talent died.

Meg came home for Easter her second year at school in North Carolina. She received our travel money and wired back "Money received. Going like water. PS I still

have seven more words. I love each one of you all."

I knew the date she would arrive but not the hour, so I kept a golf date instead of waiting at home. Meg came to the course to look for me. I saw her two holes away just as she saw me. We ran toward each other like that old teevee commercial. It was a dear moment.

That year Meg was visited at St. Genevieve by an illustrious man with an illustrious nickname, the holder of an exalted position with a lowly title. He was Fishbait Miller, doorkeeper of the US House of Representatives. That lowly title is given to the person without whom the House could not operate. He was in charge of 300 House personnel from the pages to the police and the men and women who perform the duties that enable the House to operate. The public knows him only as the unnamed man who enters the legislative chambers and bawls out the names of visiting dignitaries, including the President. Fishbait was W. M. Miller but hardly anyone knew that.

While driving from Washington back to his Pascagoula home, Fishbait stopped off at

Meg's school. As he was leaving, Mother Potts and Meg walked with him to his car. Meg said that Fishbait put his arm around Mother Potts' shoulder and told her, "Now mother honey, you take good care of this little girl Meg, you hear?"

Meg said she "nearly died" at the hug but "I think Mother Potts really enjoyed it."

Meg's life after high school seemed more soap opera than that of other people's, but we will skip the teary parts. Things eventually settled and life smoothed out for her. Pushed by her mother Meg made a brief debut during the New Orleans 1961 season. She hated every minute of it. She was presented at the first major ball. "The whole thing," she said, "was too pretentious, a waste of time and money."

Cheerful, fun loving and popular, without politicking, Meg was elected president of her sophomore and junior classes at St. Genevieve and her freshman class at Loyola.

During her last year at St. Genevieve and some time after, she attended mass daily and yearned to become a nun. She was dissuaded by Mother Potts who thought her desire was not a confirmed vocation but a romantic girlish dream. Meg's mother also disapproved and asked Meg to spend a year at college and then decide. Meg went to college and decided in eight months. She met Loren E. Bosarge, a Pascagoula native and physics graduate of Louisiana State University. They married in 1961, after Meg made the brief debut. She and Loren have two daughters.

After a divorce in 1980, Meg finished a BS and earned a master's in psychological counseling at which she worked in several practices before founding her own. In 1992 she married Richard L. Walters of Belleville, Illinois, a retired manager of a national telephone company unit. Meg retired in 2000. She and Dick live in Gautier, across the river from Pascagoula.

Maybin

HEREWITH MAYBIN'S TALE

From the age of three, Maybin the Menace was inventor of a series of the dangest mischief tricks ever devised by the mind of man. Or boy.

He was born 30 January 1947 in Baptist Hospital at New Orleans, the third boy, fourth child in the family. He rose from his cradle to apply his considerable intelligence to driving everybody around him stark, raving nuts. Sturdily built, he grew upward rapidly, as if going to catch Erik twice as old at seven. Using a formula published in a newspaper, we calculated he would be six feet, four inches tall. He stopped at five feet nine, matching the tallest known Harkey. He looked just like me.

Was there a budding Lothario on hand? At five he said he was in love with a neighboring girl, "We kiss together every day." He early had an eye for nature. "Daddy," he shouted one day, "look at all those chickens." He pointed to a flock of birds pecking along the sand bar. "Those aren't chickens, Maybin," I said, "they're sea gulls."

"Segars, Maybin exclaimed, "why aren't they on fire?"

Sammy, our black spaniel-type dog, limped home one day with a gash on his haunch. The fight started when a "big yellow dog stuck his tongue out at Sammy," Maybin explained. I have no idea where Maybin got the inspiration for this next. Maybe it sprang from his own developing bossman personality. At three, he called out at 7:30 p.m. one evening, "Daddy come kiss me good night and turn out the light and get outa here and close the door." Daddy complied.

He was listening to a radio one Sunday afternoon, broke off to run and tell me, "Daddy come listen. I've got Jesus and god!"

One afternoon when he was four, I couldn't get his attention even by bellowing at him from across the room. "Can't you hear me, Maybin?" I called twice. "No, this ear's broke and don't work any more."

Even as a toddler he reveled in new places, new corners to investigate, new spots to hide. There never was a lad so young to be in charge on his environment. Things usually happened to others. Maybin happened to things. Discovering chocolate milk, one morning he intercepted the milkman and ordered chocolate milk to replace the white milk every day. All drank brown milk for a while.

Deciding to be a policeman, at four he went into traffic on Beach Boulevard and flagged down several trucks and autos. Genuine cops sirened up to investigate the hair raising reports phoned in by nearly hysterical citizens. One year our house was included in those open to tours on a garden club's annual "pilgrimage." The guest book bore names of visitors from 11 other states and Canada, and prominent among signatures was "Mr. Maybin Harkey, Pascagoula, Mississippi."

The year before he was to start school Maybin had a best friend whose temperament and personality were much like his own. This was Benjy Best. At a PTA meeting one teacher whispered (not soft enough) to another, "Just think next year we get Benjy Best."

"That's not all," replied the other. "Don't you know we also get Maybin Harkey."

When he was five he was enrolled at a pre-kindergarten school where he took over games and swaggered around like Arnold Schwartzenegger until he ran across two boys as tough as he. He decided he didn't like school. That night, though, he asked Mama for extra candy to take to school. Next day he distributed candy kisses all around, with largest hauls going to the two toughies. It was an incredibly sophisticated display for a child.

An active tree climber, runner, lifter, thrower, Maybin turned into a fine athlete but never used his abilities. At thirteen he entered a high school football game briefly as a running back. On his first carry he took off at such speed that everybody including the opposing players gasped. He played two years. He was second in breath holding at a swimming meet, a talent we tried to have him practice at home.

Maybin wanted to be included in every group that Erik and Meg joined. He raged because the school music director did not chose him also for a tyro instrumental class. The school did not have the instrument that Maybin might be most interested in, a steam calliope.

Rough-tough Maybin, ready to dive head first into any dispute, was a softie about animals. He was gentle with all, brought home a succession of misfit dogs, cats, even a bird. He thought all were beautiful. A dog he called Yellow was so unsightly that it is impossible to describe. Words fail.

One of Maybin's true talents was eating. When he was twelve he spent a night with a friend. The father told me that he kept piling vittles on Maybin's breakfast plate – eggs, bacon, sausage, nine pancakes – and asked him, "How's that Maybin?"

"Where's the toast?"

Unexplained things happened around Maybin. When he was four, we awakened to find a window shade by his bed in shreds and tatters. "The skeeters did it, Daddy." We never found out how monstrous mosquitos had managed to evade the Air Force radar curtain.

At nine, Maybin went with brother Erik, twelve, to a summer camp in North Carolina. We were mildly surprised that Maybin, always rapt in his private concerns, felt a touch of home sickness, In a letter to Bobi, oldest sibling at seventeen, he wrote, "Miss you very much. I bet your glad that I left for camp. Up here is not home. Wish I was home because I miss the hold family."

The "hold" family sorely missed him. When he left home Mama told brother Erik to help keep him out of trouble. Impossible. Erik wrote home, "I don't see Maybin much but I can hear him."

Indeed. Maybin was eminently hearable, even in a crowd. When he left the crowd, it was like a mob dispersing. He wrote, "I'm having fun but I'm getting in too much trouble." Some sort of social crisis must have caused him to ask that a hundred pieces of "dubble bubble gum" be sent immediately. Camp rules were taking a hideous beating. Erik's final report was depressing.

"I'm sorry to say I have some bad news on Maybin," Erik wrote. "He has been docked 10 to 11 times and acts like a jurk. He already has spent about $13 in the camp bank. He buys all kinds of junk. He has lost his tennis racket and his brown loafers. He got this knife that somebody gave him and he throws it all over the place, in trees, in chair and I don't know what else. I finally had to take it away from him."

After camp, back at school, Maybin continued his free style behavior. Whenever a strange unscheduled event occurred – say, a snarl arises, a crisis develops, a squabble breaks out, a pigtail is yanked, the cry is sounded "Maybin did it." Zoe Belle Cox, much loved third grade teacher at Beach School, said she was tired of hearing that cry and from then on would call Maybin by his first name, Lewis. Maybin is now used only by the family.

Maybin finished high school in North Carolina and joined the Marine Corp on a program of boot camp and a hitch in the Reserves. I knew nothing of all that, as I'd not heard from him for months. It was a surprise when at age 18 he showed up in Pascagoula aboard a "giant motorcycle". He told me he wanted $5,000 to go to California to surf. He was outfitted for a motorcycle life – black leather with metal studs, greasy hair down to the shoulders, jack boots. "Gimme five thousand, Pop," he said again, "and I'll be on my way." I said I had to think about it.

He moved into his mother's home and I saw little of him for months. When I did see him he asked again for money to go to California. I had worked out what I'd decided. It was that he go to New Orleans and spend a week with a psychological testing service which had been recommended to me. "They will find your aptitudes and your achievements so far and tell us what they indicate you should do with your life."

He decided to return to his mother's. A few weeks later he told me he wanted to take my offer of psychological evaluation. The core of the recommendation by the psychologists was that he go to college and study accounting. Glory be! He had agreed to undergo the study, now he was accepting the recommendation. He enrolled in the Jesuit school, Spring Hill College at Mobile. During his four years there he followed a precarious course of alternating probations with semesters in good standing. For one semester he would draw 1.8 as GPA and be placed on probation. Next semester he would score high enough to lose the probation tag and bring his average up to good standing for a semester, then back to probation.

It was a precarious existence, flirting with expulsion every other semester. Pity was that a student of genuine scholarly ability could have done this trick, and Maybin was just playing with his talent.

On graduating he went to work at Ingalls Shipbuilding at Pascagoula, the state's largest industrial establishment in the cost accounting department. Afterward there were jobs and ownership of a boat company and a restaurant motel. With his first wife Maybin was father of a daughter and a son. He and his fifth wife live in Pascagoula.

INTERLUDE: A CHRISTMAS TALE

It was a long time before the storm hit our house. It wasn't named Arthur, Benny or Chuck, but all in one Erik, Maybin, Amelie, and Dale. Like a hurricane standing off shore and picking up strength by the minute, my people for about ten days had been building up anticipation until they were about ready to burst.

It was Christmas morning. The storm struck before dawn with a fury. Two segments, called Bobi and Meg, skirted us without damage.

Aftermath was a large room that looked as if Genghis Khan had passed through. Mountains of torn and balled up paper, string, cards and already dismembered toys covered the floor and all the furniture, no longer identifiable. Shrieks, laughs, singing, arguments, ringing bells, tooting horns supplied sound effects. The poor little tree, stripped of its gay decorations, sagged forlornly in its corner.

Frazzled parents, worn but still able to enjoy the children enjoying, tried to direct the chaos for a while then gave up. After all, it's Christmas, so what the heck.

Erik and Maybin, during a truce, did their shopping together and decided that each should give the other a rubber knife. The sword fight began. Erik gave big brother a pair of pink sox, not shocking pink but staggering pink.

One present under the tree was not marked with a card. "Don't know whose this is," I said, holding it up. "There's no card with it."

"That's mine," seven year old Erik said.

"Well, it doesn't say who it's from," I said.

"It's from me," Erik said. "I wanted a second knife so I gave me one."

Erik's gifts to his siblings, though, all bore cards. They read "of Rik to Meg," "of Rik to Bobi" and so on. I asked Rik what the "of Rik" meant. "I don't know how to spell from," he explained, "so I put of."

"Now," I continued "one of these reads 'of Rik to Mo.' Who is Mo?"

"Simple," said Rik. "I didn't know how to spell Maybin either, so I wrote Mo."

Bobi gave me three cans of tobacco. Meg gave me two handkerchiefs. Rik said his gift for me was first intended for his teacher Miss Mitchell, "But they said not to give teachers anything, so I gave them to you. You can put them on your desk in the office."

They were something I had yearned for over many years. Three boxes of Roundheads No 4 Steel Paper Fasteners. They went on my desk that evening.

Erik at nine

HEREWITH ERIK'S TALE

There were a dozen policemen in our yard, milling about, wielding flash lights in the dark, examining bushes and shrubs and hidden corners. All that was missing for a forensic convention was Magnum, Mannix, Peter Gunn, Perry Mason or Columbo.

Erik was missing also.

No one had seen the five year old for about six hours. It was 11p.m., long after Erik had been expected home for dinner and bed. The force was in our yard. Sheriff Guy Krebs, deputy Leo Byrd and others were scouring the huge yard of our rented home. With arrival of Pascagoula acting Chief Foster

Barrow and assistant chief Troy Parker and several city officers, the top guns of Jackson County were present. They began planning a canvass of neighboring homes.

Slim, yellow haired Erik knew that he was to log in at home every day before dark. He had a wrist watch, but he had not yet conquered the habit of looking at it. With an officer, I spent an hour under the blazing portable lights on site and scaring the wits out of neighbors who opened their doors to find The Law calling. I tried to keep my fear from turning into panic. A dear little boy was missing. Where was he? What had happened to him? While we searched, his mother was inside the house phoning everyone who may have seen Erik since five o'clock.

All of a sudden, there was Erik.

He was walking through the backyard toward the house, rubbing his eyes, dirty as a little boy. "What's all the people doing in our yard," he asked. "And all those lights."

I sucked in a full breath and yelled, "WHERE HAVE YOU BEEN?"

He'd hidden under a bush nearby two hours before, to watch, he said, but had fallen asleep. He was awakened when more men came and the noise increased. My fear disappeared under relief and a flush of anger was washed away when I grabbed and hugged him.

Erik was born 12 June 1944 in New Orleans when I was a Navy lieutenant (jg). He was notable for a full head of coal black hair in a family of blonds. At nine pounds six ounces, he was the largest at birth. He also was born at Baptist Hospital.

I first saw Erik for a few minutes after passing through New Orleans en route to San Francisco for shipping out. He looked just like me. The infant Erik, his mother, Bobi and Meg were at the Levert summer house at Biloxi. I drove to see him and to tell all goodbye.

Many children flee when grownups come calling. Not Erik. He stayed and mingled with them, learning as a very young boy how they talked and acted. The experience added a confidence to his manner that was most notable in contrast to the manners of others of his under ten-age.

One of his habits worried me, however. After our guests had left, Erik would circle the room, drinking the dregs in each glass. I strove to quash that habit, because there was alcoholism in all the families from which he descended. I was not very successful, but Erik did not acquire the families' curse.

At age four, still living in New Orleans, Rik attended St. Marks Episcopal Church kindergarten around the corner from our Coliseum Street home. He always came home representing an animal, creeping, crawling, slinking, making appropriate sounds. One day he crawled into the living room making growling noises but ended the performance abruptly and ran. When he came back I asked, "What was that, Rik, a goat?"

"No," he answered, "that tiger had to pee."

He occasionally paid the price of a paddling by his mother. Maybin, a spectator one day, admonished his mother, "Mama, you shouldn't do that to people."

Erik entered Beach School in 1950. His first morning he and his mother looked over the house trying to find at least one of his two pairs of shoes. No luck. He showed up for his inaugural classes wearing blue and red slippers two sizes too big.

Teachers and principal had a job trying to break Rik of a habit of yelling to Meg when he passed her classes. Meg told us of one incident. "He came by the door of my classroom and yelled, 'Hey, Meg, I'm going to get a drink of water.'"

Five year old Erik was very fond of a pony ring where he used to ride. Passing it one day in the auto he pointed out a lady pony and made the announcement, "She laid a little colt yesterday."

At ten Erik wanted to join Meg and learn to play the piano. As he plugged away I noticed he did a fairly good "One Blind Mouse." I noted in my newspaper, "Maybe he can add the other two mice soon and be able to play the entire composition." Later he tried the trumpet but was stopped. Must have been by the board of health.

Also at ten Rik had his first date. Rather, his first half date Jane Quinn asked him to take her to her Girl Scout dance. She asked George Tomlinson also. Rik and George are best friends to this date.

That same year Erik's sense of responsibility earned him the coveted honor

of escorting every day Beach Schools'
lunchroom money to school headquarters.
He made a show of the trip, with a little red
radio attached to his bike, blaring out the
depressing "music" of the day.

Erik did not seek leadership but he was
ready when it was thrust upon him. Also at
ten, he was invited to attend a Sunday supper
meeting of a Presbyterian church youth
group. Back home we asked him how the
affair went. "Fine," he said, "I'm president."

"WHAT?"

"They elected me president."

"But, Erik, you don't belong to that group
and you're not even a member of that church."

I checked. The woman in charge of girls
and boys groups said she pointed out that to
the boys. They said Erik's a 'good man' and
they wanted him to be president. I didn't
interfere and I never learned how the
Presbyterian club fared under the leadership
of a Roman Catholic.

Early in his high school days, I put Erik
to work at my newspaper as a sports writer.
He did fine for a while and then one day at
deadline I looked everywhere for Erik's
copy. No copy. No reason, he said, just

didn't do it. He wouldn't tell me why, wouldn't blame outside foul-ups. But I thought it would do him good, so I fired him. Maybin, working in the back shop, quit. I couldn't persuade him to see that his move was a non sequitur, not a proper response to Erik's ousting.

Erik, with all the qualities of a ladies man, did do well in the dating field. He graduated from University of Mississippi. With his talents, a sense of humor and a positive attitude, Erik enjoyed popularity through high school and college.

After college, with the talents and savvy of an entrepreneur, he held a variety of jobs before entering the fast food industry in 1983. A workaholic, he owned seven outlets when he sold his hamburger holdings in 2003. He immediately began scouting to buy several small businesses that he could run by himself with small staffs.

Erik married soon after college graduation, divorced. He married again. He and his second wife Betty have two sons and live in Columbia, Mississippi, about a hundred miles inland from the Gulf Coast. He is the only Harkey offspring not anchored to the Coast.

Dale at five

HEREWITH DALE'S TALE

No. 6, a beautiful little boy, did no dawdling en route, and arrived at Jackson County Hospital on 12 September 1952, only 16 months behind Amelie.

Reactions among the family were varied. Mother's reservations about bringing forth a sixth child turned to delight when she saw what she had produced and the obvious delight of the father. Bobi and Erik were satisfied because, thinking well ahead, they saw help with their responsibilities. Meg was disappointed because she had no new little living doll to play with. Lee toddled, unaware that she was no longer The Baby. Maybin's reaction was widely different. He was disgusted.

He had tried to do some advance work by asking neighbor Doyle Berry, "You want a baby when it comes to our house? We got too many kids running around the house now."

The newcomer was called Baby X as I climbed family trees in search of names. A traditionalist, I believe family names should be given newcomers. You won't find a Madonna Harkey or Iced-T Harkey around here. William was my paternal grandfather. Another William Millsaps was a veteran of the War of 1812. Millsaps was my paternal grandmother's maiden name, Trousdale, my maternal great-grandmother's.

A whole lot of names to place on an unsuspecting infant.

Until Amelie was three she had trouble classifying the new baby. It's not a toy because it cries when you poke a finger in its eye. It's not a real person because all it does is lie in bed all day. Grownups kiss it and afterward make curious sounds. After Amelie kisses it she gives it a little slap.

Baby X, now William Millsaps Trousdale Harkey was yowling like fury when he was carried from the hospital. He was beautiful even in rage and looked just like me. Mrs.

Reddick, his nurse who was carrying him said he was protesting "because of all those names you gave him." I thought, Millsaps in Mississippi and Trousdale in Tennessee may be of great comfort to him some day.

To help with raising the new baby a new nurse was hired. Six feet, coal black skin, most pleasant face. This was Clementine, of the beautiful soul, who came to love all the children and all of us loved her. The first time I saw her she was pedaling Meg's bicycle at full speed around the yard with Amelie gleefully hanging on in the wire basket.

Three years later Dale, as we now called him, bloomed with a head of brilliant yellow curls. Some said it was a shame that Amelie, the girl, had rigidly straight hair while the boy Dale displayed his yellow curls. In his buggy, Dale was going to be a sure magnet for cooing strangers.

At three, though, other things were on his mind. A neighbor bought a yard full of chickens. At dawn each morning a rooster greeted the sun with raucous voice. First day Dale asked, "Mama, what is he barking at?"

Dale was answering the phone when he was four. Returning from a trip, I phoned

home from New Orleans. Dale answered.
"How have you been, Dale?"

"Fine."

"Have you been a good boy?"

"What?"

"Have you been a good boy while I was away?"

Pause. Long silence. Then.

"Who is this?"

Teevee captured Dale when he was four.
"Daddy, guess how I want to taste," he posed.
Puzzled, I asked, "How?" He said, "Like a cigarette
should." Damn television. One night he wouldn't
say his prayers. When I asked he said, "I got tired
of moving my lips." Strange boy.

An irked-amused woman told me that
Dale answered our phone when she called
and told her that his Mama had gone "to play
bridge with some old ladies." Caller was the
head of the "old ladies" bridge club.

At age five, more teevee influence. Dale's
favorite song which he sang incessantly for
two days was, "You get a lot to like in a
mullberry – fitter, fwavor, fwip top box."
Standing naked before the locked bathroom
door, five-year-old Dale said, "Let me in, Lee.
Daddy said to let me in or he'll spank you."
He used the name of authority in vain, I hadn't

told him anything. From inside, Amelie called, "That's just silly. If you can't get in, how can he get in to spank me."

The cast of a school play was milling around making a lot of noise at rehearsal. The thorns were behaving in a most unthorn-like manner. "For heaven's sake," called the lady director, "you thorns get back in line and keep still. We're about to go on. Quiet!"

Suddenly Dale, a thorn, emitted an ear piercing shriek. "Now what's the matter, Dale? Can't you obey?" To which Dale answered quietly, "You're standing on my foot."

After a Senior Bowl game, we stopped for refreshments at a Mobile restaurant.

Dale asked me to order hot chocolate for him while he wandered off to inspect things nine-year-old boys wander off to inspect instead of waiting for the waitress.

When Dale returned I told him the restaurant did not have hot chocolate so we ordered him hot vanilla instead.

"Hot vanilla," he shouted. He protested stoutly that he did not, repeat not, definitely did not want a cup of hot vanilla.

The laughter of the rest of us turned into an explosion when Dale's order was put before him. A marshmallow atop the steaming liquid in his cup had melted, the liquid was white and Dale nearly choked because he thought sure enough a cup of "hot vanilla" had been placed before him.

At six years, Amelie had a ready reason why Dale, only five is taller than she. "Dale has a long, tall head like Maybin," she told me, "and I have a fat head like you." Saints forbid.

At seven Dale had a small speck in the middle of his upper gum line. A new tooth budding, but it won't make up for the three recently lost. Eating at a restaurant with big brother Erik and me, Dale was last in the gulping race. Blanche, our waitress said, "Why Dale, you sure are slow."

Dale's response, "I don't have much teeth."

At eight, Dale's long silent stretches were more noticeable than ever. I asked him, "You sure don't talk much, do you Dale?"

"No," he replied, "but I watch a lot."

So there is Dale as a young boy. He was a high school and college Romeo, handsome. That is not my judgment alone but that of dozens of young and older girls and women. In college he had to date carefully in certain ways to prevent warfare among contending groups.

He grew into a six-foot specimen, half a foot taller than I. He was graduated from Spring Hill College at Mobile. Hearing of large sums being paid workers in Texas oilfields, he went west for a job.

He worked here and there and the handsome pay kept him there for more than a year. He began noticing that "old men" of 50-55 years who had been at it for years were making only a little more in real money than when they had started.

Let's move on he suggested to his lifelong friend Richard Chenoweth who has accompanied Dale since high school. Dale decided to move on to law school at the University of Mississippi. He did well at studies and magnificently in the dating game until he met the fine young woman who became his wife. He and Barbara Houston Harkey live in Pascagoula with their son William and daughter Marielle.

Dale, the quiet listener, is now in his second term as district circuit judge for three counties in southeast Mississippi. His record for probity is attested by the fact that he ran unopposed in his last elections for district attorney and then judge. (Vote for Dale!)

Kathy visits

HEREWITH KATHY'S TALE

There is a seventh Harkey, Katherine, in the crowd. Kathy joined the assembly in 1975, too late to take part in the moving experience to Pascagoula. She was born April 12, 1968, in Florida and came to us when she was seven, so tiny that she often was turned back by school teachers when she went to her classes. They thought she was an out-of-place kindergartner.

Kathy was raised by her mother in Massachusetts, was graduated from the University of Connecticut. Married and divorced at the time this book appeared, she was a successful marketer of computer programs for attorneys.

A lovely, willowy 5-9 blonde, Kathy lives in Chicago.

"Susy investigates" " Sammy follows"

HEREWITH
ANIMAL TALES

Sammy, our black dog, was a passionate auto rider, but not for the usual canine pleasure of taking in the air.

For Sammy, a ride in a car was an ego-bolstering experience that allowed him for a few moments to compensate for his natural feelings of inferiority.

Sammy, you see, was a gentle dog, almost a sissy dog, but from the seat of a car he could be ferocious as he wanted without fear of retribution. Hanging half way out the window, at everything that moved, he would snarl like a tiger, bark in a frenzy and lunge about like a harpooned whale, as if he would give his right paw to get out and get at 'em.

Once, when he was giving this terrifying treatment to a startled pedestrian dog we were passing, I stopped the car and opened the door on Sammy's side.

Sammy's blood thirstiness evaporated and he fell onto the seat as limp as a wet bathing suit, top dog no more.

This was, I admit, a cruel way to humiliate Sammy, such a sweet dog. But I wanted to check my estimate of his character and this was a good way to do it. Nobody knows but Sammy and me and I can keep a secret.

*   *   *

On Ford Avenue near S. Pascagoula lived a former wheel chasing dog. The animal, heavy with the weight of years, usually lay at the edge of the street near his driveway. As a car approached he flattened out on the ground like a snake, moving his head to keep the vehicle in sight. His ancient muscles twitched, but except for his head he remained motionless.

Old eyes sparked as he took vicarious joy, scowling at the car until it no longer was a threat to his home territory. I often went out of my way to drive down Ford Avenue to give that old boy a chance to work his adrenals while returning in memory to the dashing thrills of his youth.

*   *   *

Exodus week has been observed at our place. Squeeker's kittens were old enough to leave mama and sally forth to seek their fortunes in the world.

The process was an emotional wrench I hadn't anticipated.

It started about 5:30p.m. when Catherine Ford walked into the yard carrying a box lined with a blanket. She, with Meg's help, picked out the black and yellow speckled kitten we called Mole. (His nose, from eyes to tip, is a yellow strip in a field of black, giving him a startling resemblance to a star-nosed mole.)

Catherine walked off home with Mole. Meg, eleven, watched and began weeping. She wailed that the kittens were so cute, she wanted to keep them, they'd miss their mother, that Squeeker would be desolate without them.

We countered with the fact that all creatures must grow up and eventually leave their homes, their mothers; that's when Meg got Squeeker, the kitten only a few weeks old, younger than her own kittens now.

The sobbing gradually ceased, but Meg remained red-eyed and morose. Suddenly a wail louder than ever pierced the evening calm. "Now here comes Gay for HER kitten," Meg howled, the tears squirting.

Sure enough, Gay Kihyet was prancing up the drive, a box under her arm. To the obligato of pure heartbreak from Meg. Gay picked out a solid black, very fluffy number and took it home. Things were lachrymose at our place for some time.

* * *

I was driving one evening when, from under a street light, a black and white cat darted away from a shadow in the middle of the street and ran to the shoulder. It ran in spurts, hesitantly, stopped at the street edge and looked back.

As I rolled closer I saw that the shadow wasn't a shadow. It was a tiny, tar-black kitten. I stopped and got out of the car. The kitten rose and began tottering on newborn legs, yowling four times as big as itself. It flopped in fear as I drew close.

The adult cat began creeping toward the kitten. She would creep close then flee because of me. She was torn between her need to retrieve junior and her fear of the human.

I got back in the car, moved to the street edge and watched. Mama streaked to Junior and it danced wobbly but blissfully while she spruced it up with her gentle tongue. Then she took the kitten in her mouth and bore it across the road to the shadows to safety. All instinct, of course, because everybody knows cats have no souls.

Susy on guard

Squeeker relaxing

Bobi, "four". Meg "two"

Meg at three

Shown above and seated from left, Meg at 14; Dale, two; Amelie, three; Bobi at 16. Standing are Erik, 11; Maybin at 8

AFTERWORD

When I came home from China in late 1945, a college professor told me that a student had written a story about my daughter Meg when Meg was four years old during the last year of World War II. Meg was only one year old when I left for Navy duty and had no memory of me. Sometimes when she saw a man in uniform she would run up to him, look up and ask, "Are you my Daddy?"